Now I Can Hear!

by Connie Losacano

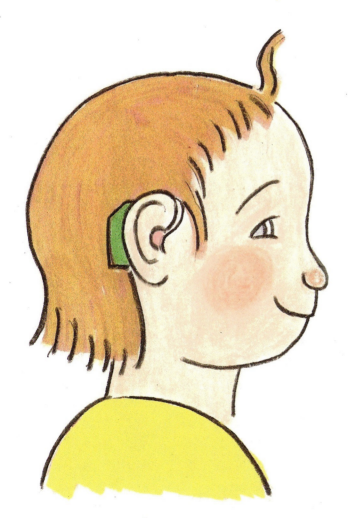

AuthorHouse™
1663 Liberty Drive
Bloomington, IN 47403
www.authorhouse.com
Phone: 1-800-839-8640

© 2009 Connie Losacano. All rights reserved.

No part of this book may be reproduced, stored in a retrieval system, or transmitted by any means without the written permission of the author.

First published by AuthorHouse 12/1/2009

ISBN: 978-1-4490-5270-6 (sc)

Printed in the United States of America
Bloomington, Indiana

This book is printed on acid-free paper.

I can't hear some sounds,

because my ears do not work very well.

I wear hearing aids to help me hear better.

I am so happy because

and the sound of

a bird singing.

and the sound of

a sheep.

and the sound of

tick tock

a clock.

Now I can hear

a big, red train

and best of all, the sound of Mommy saying

I love you!